Classical Literature

Comprehension Activities to Develop Interest in Reading

Grades 5–6

Written by
George Moore

Published by World Teachers Press®

Order Number 2-5174
ISBN 1-58324-101-9

A B C D E F 03 02 01 00

Educational Resources
395 Main Street
Rowley, MA 01969
www.worldteacherspress.com

Foreword

The story summaries featured in this book are derived from classic tales which have delighted children and adults for generations. Even if the children in today's schools have not read the original stories, they have met some of fiction's greatest characters through feature films, full-length cartoons and television series based on these classic books. Film makers from different eras are constantly returning to these classics because their storylines are so interesting, so it is hoped children in schools today will also be familiar with our rich literary heritage and will, at some time in their lives, read these great books and those from other countries around the world.

Table of Contents

Teachers Notes

A lot of reading provided for students reflects modern society and the interests and views of contemporary educators and students alike. It is becoming more recognized that this form of reading, while being appropriate to modern-day society, does not provide any history of reading, writers, or of authors themselves. Many authors of the past wrote material that can best be described as "Classic." This book aims to bring students a taste of the "Classics" so that their interest and imagination can be sparked to encourage them to read more Classical Literature.

By investigating Classical Literature it can be argued:

(a) That literature can be based on actuality or fantasy and includes written and oral texts, films, plays, poems, novels, legends, biographies, etc.

(b) That students should study literature from other countries which has been translated into English.

(c) That through reading and critically responding to literature, students extend their understanding of the world and themselves.

(d) That a wide range of literature should be available and should include shared experiences such as those experienced when a class enjoys a video or a teacher's reading as a group.

(e) That examination of the different values of other times is important in the study of literature stories/topics.

(f) That classic literature refers to works recognized over time as excellent examples of their type.

The summaries of the stories are open-ended to encourage children to read the suggested junior fiction books and discover for themselves what happens.

The stories are sequenced in an approximate order of difficulty and teachers notes are provided.

The "R" at the bottom of every story page denotes additional reading and literature appreciation activities.

Teachers Notes

❖ Finite Verbs

A finite verb is a verb with a subject. In the examples below, the basic sentences are not italicized and contain the finite verbs limited to their subjects. The past participle (dressed) and the present participle (riding) are not complete verbs and introduce adjectival phrases which describe the nouns "lady" and "boy" and help to improve the basic sentence.

e.g.   The lady *dressed in black* smiled at her friend.
  (subject)   (phrase)   (verb)

The boy *riding the bicycle* raced down the street.
  (subject)   (phrase)   (verb)

❖ Adjectival Clauses

An adjectival clause (a descriptive group of words containing a verb) describes a noun or pronoun. This type of clause usually begins with the relative pronouns "who," "which," "whose," or "whom" (so named because they relate to a noun or pronoun already used in the sentence). The relative pronoun can be substituted as the subject of the clause by the noun/pronoun it describes but the original clause is only a subordinate clause as it does not make complete sense by itself.

e.g.   The sailor *who boarded the ship* was very young.
    (adjectival clause)

Adjectival clauses are often introduced by a preposition governing the relative pronoun.

e.g.   We opened the chest *in* which the gold was hidden.

She held the baby *for* whom she felt so much pity.

He liked Tony *at* whose house he often stayed.

❖ Adverbial Clauses

An adverbial clause (a group of words containing a verb) adds further meaning to a verb. The most common types are adverb clauses of time, place and reason. They usually follow the verb they modify.

e.g.   (a)   He could leave after he had finished the test.
    When? After he had finished the test. (time)
  (b)   The book was placed where everyone could see it.
    Where? Where everyone could see it. (place)
  (c)   She smiled because she had won a prize.
    Why? Because she had won a prize. (reason)

❖ Prepositional Phrases

A prepositional phrase is a group of words which does not contain a verb and begins with a preposition (e.g. *on* the table, *near* the tree). Depending on its position in the sentence it can be an adjectival phrase usually describing a noun already used or an adverb phrase usually following a verb.

e.g.   Adjectival: The book *on the bed* is mine. (Not any book but the book on the bed.)

Adverbial: She slept *on the bed*. (Where? On the bed - adverb phrase of place.)
He came *after dark*. (When? After dark - adverb phrase of time.)
She flew *like a bird*. (How? Like a bird - adverb phrase of manner.)

Astrid Lindgren has been a popular writer of children's books since her fantasy "Pippi Longstrump" was published in 1945. Her character, Pippi, who plans to be a pirate when she grows up, represents every child's dream of the freedom to do as one pleases. Pippi's story has been translated into many languages.

Pippi Longstocking

Pippi is a nine-year-old girl who lives in a small town in Sweden. She is an orphan as her mother has died and her father, a ship's captain, has disappeared at sea.

Pippi has reddish hair braided in two braids which stand out at right angles to her head and a cute freckled nose. On her thin legs she wears one black and one brown stocking and on her feet, black shoes which are much too big. This unusual, horseriding girl wears a blue dress covered with red patches. She is strong enough to lift her horse and on her shoulder sits a clothed monkey called Mr. Nelson.

Before vanishing, Pippi's father had bought an old cottage in an orchard for his retirement. When Pippi decides to live there, she befriends two children, Tommy and Annika, who live next door. The townspeople hear about the young girl living alone and decide she must be placed in a children's home. However, Pippi gets the better of the two policemen who come to take her away!

Later, Tommy and Annika persuade her to attend school, where she totally disrupts a math lesson. Pippi then organizes a picnic for her three friends and amazes them when she deals with a bull which threatens to spoil their outing. On a visit to a circus, Pippi upsets the bareback rider and a tightrope walker. She takes part in their acts to the delight of the audience who clap and cheer her. She even defeats the circus's strongman in a wrestling match! When two thieves plan to rob Pippi, she outwits them. Then, to their dismay, she forces them to dance a polka with her until the early hours of the morning. They are so glad to leave! On another occasion, with Mr. Nelson's assistance, she is praised as a heroine by the townspeople and two young boys are eternally grateful to her. I wonder why?

Read one of these junior fiction books:

Pippi Longstocking – Astrid Lindgren
Pippi Goes on Board – Astrid Lindgren
Pippi in the South Seas – Astrid Lindgren

Pippi Longstocking

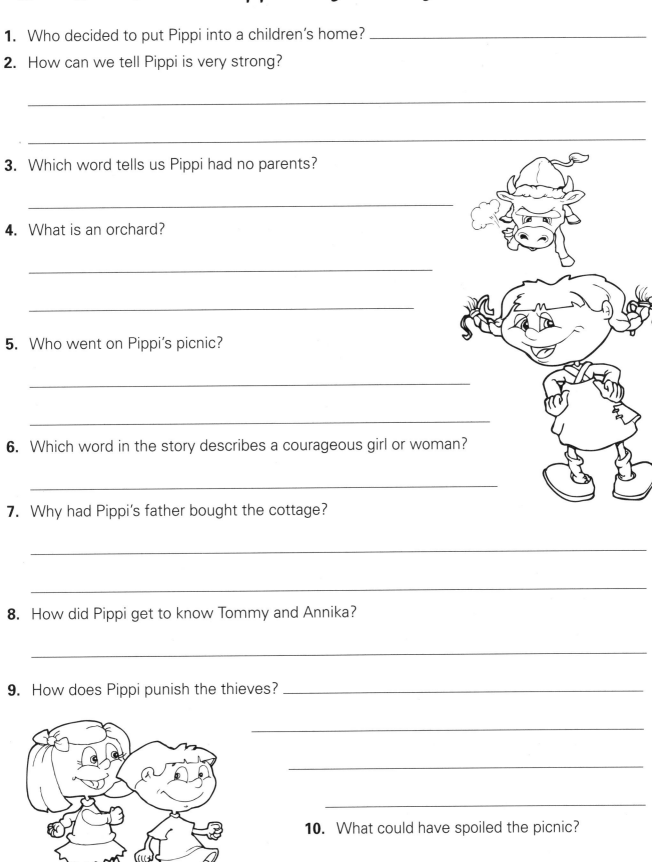

1. Who decided to put Pippi into a children's home? _____

2. How can we tell Pippi is very strong?

_____

_____

3. Which word tells us Pippi had no parents?

_____

4. What is an orchard?

_____

_____

5. Who went on Pippi's picnic?

_____

_____

6. Which word in the story describes a courageous girl or woman?

_____

7. Why had Pippi's father bought the cottage?

_____

_____

8. How did Pippi get to know Tommy and Annika?

_____

_____

9. How does Pippi punish the thieves? _____

_____

_____

10. What could have spoiled the picnic?

_____

_____

Pippi Longstocking

1. Use the information in the story to draw a picture of Pippi Longstocking in the space alongside.

   Then view the video *The New Adventures of Pippi Longstocking* and retell one of her adventures in your own words.

2. Number these events from the story in correct time order.

   (a)   Pippi's father disappears at sea.

   (b)   The circus audience claps for Pippi.

   (c)   Pippi's father buys the cottage.

   (d)   Pippi meets Annika and Tommy.

   (e)   Policemen come to take Pippi away.

3. A fantasy is a highly imaginative story in which impossible things happen. Check the examples which show this story is a fantasy.

   (a)   A girl has a pet monkey.

   (b)   A nine-year-old girl lives alone.

   (c)   A young girl can lift a horse.

   (d)   A girl disrupts a math lesson.

   (e)   Pippi beats a strongman at wrestling.

4. Complete this passage with your own words (some could be found in the story). Use one word in each space.

   Because she is so _____ and can _____ a horse, Pippi is an

   _____ girl. She has a _____ for a friend and it _____

   on her shoulder. The townspeople _____ that Pippi should not live

   _____ but she does not _____ with them. At the _____

   Pippi upsets some of the performers but people in the _____ love her.

William Tell is a famous legendary hero of Switzerland. Though there is no firm evidence that such a man ever lived, early historians believed there was some truth in the stories about him. The legend has been linked to the foundation of Switzerland from several separate states.

William Tell

Hundreds of years ago near the shores of Lake Lucerne in Europe there were three small countries, now known as Switzerland. The inhabitants were happy for their lands were beautiful and there was no lack of food to eat. Then they were conquered by an emperor's soldiers from nearby Austria. The people were forced to pay unfair taxes and were treated harshly by their new rulers.

One very important person was a governor called Gessler, who was a merciless tyrant. He ordered his troops to destroy the houses and crops of those subjects who disobeyed him. Gessler even made the downtrodden people bow to his hat. It was displayed on a pole in the market square in the town of Altdorf for all to see.

Gessler was jealous of the popular William Tell, who lived up in the Alps with his wife, Hedwig, and their two sons. When William refused to bow to the hat, the evil governor threatened him with death unless he could shoot an apple off his son's head to save them both.

All the townspeople stood near and were horrified as Tell's son refused a blindfold and showed his pluck by placing the apple on his own head. Then his father took a step forward and carefully aimed his crossbow. The arrow flew through the air, splitting the apple in two—a remarkable feat. William had hidden another arrow inside his jerkin; that was intended for Gessler had William missed and slain his own son.

When Gessler realized William's plan he was furious. He had the crossbowman arrested and tied up, but his prisoner escaped and vowed revenge. Though Gessler tried to recapture him, William Tell was determined to rid the land of this wicked ruler so his people and his family would be free again. Let us hope he was successful!

Read one of these junior fiction books:

William Tell – a version illustrated by M. Early
William Tell – a version by L.E. Fisher

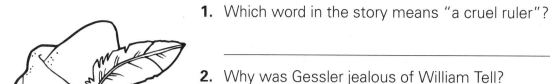

1. Which word in the story means "a cruel ruler"?

_____

2. Why was Gessler jealous of William Tell?

_____

_____

3. What silly thing did Gessler make the conquered people do?

_____

_____

4. What made Gessler very angry?

_____

5. A jerkin is a type of clothing first worn hundreds of years ago. Use a dictionary and describe what it is.

_____

6. What ruling position did Gessler occupy?

7. Write antonyms (opposites) from the story for:

(a)　pleased _____

(b)　released _____

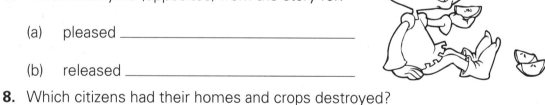

8. Which citizens had their homes and crops destroyed?

_____

9. How do we know that William Tell thought he might miss the apple and kill his son?

_____

_____

10. Why do you think the three small countries joined together to form Switzerland?

_____

_____

_____

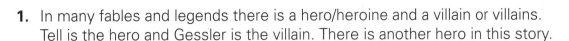

William Tell

1. In many fables and legends there is a hero/heroine and a villain or villains.
    Tell is the hero and Gessler is the villain. There is another hero in this story.

    Who is it? _____

    Why is he a hero? _____

    _____

2. On this map of part of central Europe complete these instructions.

    - On the lines provided print the capital cities of Austria and Switzerland.
    - Shade Switzerland in yellow.
    - Shade Austria in red.
    - Shade Lake Lucerne in blue.
    - Shade the Alps in brown.

3. Complete the crossword puzzle. All answers are found in the story.

    Across

1. tolls	12. shortage
2. killed	13. pace
4. deed	15. meant
6. devour	
7. envious	
9. observe	
11. very important person (abbrev.)	

    Down

1. attempted	11. promised
3. close to	14. bound
4. liberated	15. inside
5. soldiers	
7. jacket	
8. rescue	
10. courage	

4. Listen to the *William Tell Overture* by Rossini with the class. You may recognize part of the music. Research to find which TV program about another hero used this part of the overture for its theme music.

Longfellow's classic epic poem is based on the legendary stories of the Native Americans who lived along the shores of the Great Lakes in the USA. However, the real-life Hiawatha was a wise leader who lived in the eastern states of America over 500 years ago. He was chief of the Onondaga tribe and some of his exploits have become part of ancient Native American folklore.

The Song of Hiawatha

Hiawatha is a young Native American boy who is brought up in the tepee of his grandmother, Nokomis, Daughter of the Moon. Hiawatha's father, Mudjekeewis, has deserted his mother, Wenonah, who weeps at her loss and is so ill she soon lies dead of a broken heart.

Nokomis lets Hiawatha roam every trail in the pine forest which borders the shores of Gitche Gumee.

Throughout his childhood, Nokomis teaches him about the stars and comets, as they sit by their wigwam listening to the wind whispering through the leaves and the gentle lapping of waves which flow onto the

lake's shore. Hiawatha learns the language of the birds, which he calls "Hiawatha's Chickens." He is taught their names, how each bird builds its nest and where birds go in the winter. He also speaks the language of the animals, "Hiawatha's Brothers," and learns how beavers build lodges, where squirrels hide acorns, how reindeer are so swift and why the rabbit is so timid.

Later, Iagoo, a great but boastful storyteller, makes Hiawatha a bow of ash and arrows of oak from cut branches. The young brave is then told to prove his manhood by killing a deer with antlers. After his success in the hunt, the whole village celebrates with the future husband of the beautiful Minnehaha.

As Hiawatha is now a proven warrior, Nokomis decides to tell him to take revenge on her father's murderer, the powerful and merciless Megissogwon, who lives in the west and is guarded by fiery serpents. Hiawatha

takes his trusty bow, his birch canoe, his magic mittens that can crush rocks and his magic moccasins which help him to take giant strides. After he slays the serpents a fierce battle follows and one of "Hiawatha's Chickens," a kingfisher, plays an important part. Only one warrior can be victorious!

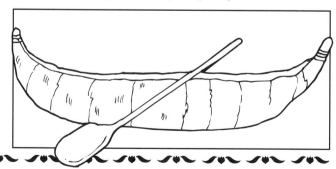

Read one of these junior fiction books:

Hiawatha – H.W. Longfellow

The Song of Hiawatha (complete poem) – H.W. Longfellow

The Song of Hiawatha

1. Gitche Gumee is a (sea, river, lake). _____

2. What is the home of a beaver called?

   _____

3. Which four trees are mentioned in the story?

   _____

   _____

   _____

4. Why was Hiawatha brought up by his grandmother?

   _____

5. Write the two names for a Native American tent used in the story.

   _____   _____

6. Who made Hiawatha's bow and arrows?

   _____

   _____

7. What sounds did Hiawatha listen to as he sat outside his home?

   _____

   _____

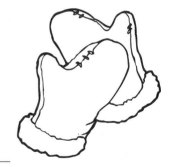

8. What were "Hiawatha's Brothers"?

   _____

9. (a) What are moccasins?

   _____

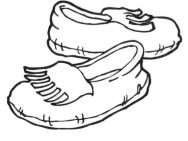

   (b) What are mittens?

   _____

10. Which word in the story can have two meanings – "courageous" or "a Native American warrior"?

   _____

The Song of Hiawatha

1. Use your imagination and write your own short story which explains why rabbits are timid or why squirrels hide acorns.

2. Using only information from the story, check matching words on this grid. One example has been done for you.

	cruel	old	brave	caring	strong	lovely	skilled	knowledgeable	young	sad
Hiawatha			✔				✔	✔	✔	
Mudjekeewis										
Nokomis										
Megissogwon										
Iagoo										
Wenonah										

3. Nouns are the names of things, persons, actions, places, etc. Select nouns from the story to complete these descriptions:

(a) _____ a collection of homes

(b) _____ a light boat

(c) _____ a large number of trees

(d) _____ a chase after prey

(e) _____ a means of communication

(f) _____ a fighting man or woman

4. Complete the crossword puzzle. All answers are found in the story.

Across

2. rejoices
4. allows
7. sobs
11. ferocious
13. a fight
14. a home
16. lifeless
19. kills
20. protected
21. move smoothly

Down

1. assist
2. lopped
3. shy
5. fast
6. tent
8. victory
9. horns
10. foliage
12. sick
15. track
17. stag
18. conceal

The god Mars is only mentioned in this story because the Romans, unlike the Greeks, did not favor legends solely about their gods. Their stories were about the Romans themselves—heroes, the early history of Rome, family relationships, etc. This is one story about the foundation of Rome.

Romulus and Remus

Two brothers, Amulius and Numitor, quarreled over who should be king of Alba Longa. Eventually the younger brother, Amulius, made himself king. He made his brother leave the kingdom and slew his sons.

Later, Amulius met his brother's beautiful daughter, Rhea Silvia. Because of her beauty, he was sure she would marry and bear children who might plan revenge against him.

Although he ordered his niece not to marry or have children, she had two sons, Romulus and Remus. Though Rhea Silvia said Mars, the god of war, was the father of her twin sons, Amulius was furious. He imprisoned the mother and commanded his servants to drown the boys in the River Tiber.

His men carried the boys to the river bank in a basket and hurriedly dumped them into the rising floodwaters.

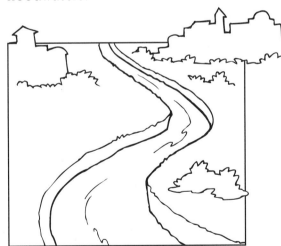

The children's cries were heard by a she-wolf, who comforted and suckled them in her cave. Then they were discovered by a needy shepherd called Faustulus, who took them back to his wife. The boys were raised by the loving couple in their humble home.

When they had grown into adults, the brothers were told how King Amulius had tried to drown them. Seeking revenge, they killed Amulius and placed their grandfather, Numitor, on the throne.

Now the brothers decided to try to build a city of their own. Unfortunately, they argued over its location. Following a sign from the gods which favored him, Romulus began building on his chosen site and decided to call his city Rome after himself. This angered Remus and the tale has a sad ending.

Read one of these junior fiction books:

Myths and Legends from Around the World – S. Shepherd
Roman Stories – Robert Hull

Romulus and Remus

1. Who was Rhea Silvia's father?

_____

2. Name the twins mentioned in the story.

_____

_____

3. Numitor was the uncle of Romulus and Remus. True or False?

_____

4. How do you think the story ends?

_____

_____

5. Which two words in the story mean "instructed"?

_____

_____

6. Who was older, Amulius or Numitor?

_____

7. In legends there is usually a hero/heroine and a villain. Who is the villain in this legend?

_____ Why? _____

_____

8. Why do you think the king's servants were in a hurry to dump the basket in the river?

_____

_____

9. Who was said to be the father of the twin boys?

_____

10. Explain the phrase "their humble home" in your own words.

_____

_____

Classical Literature

World Teachers Press®

Romulus and Remus

1. The River Tiber flows through the city of Rome.

Use your library and find out which rivers flow through these famous cities of the world.

City	River
Rome	Tiber
Paris	
New York	
London	
Cairo	
Melbourne	
Washington D.C.	
Lisbon	

2. Listed below are some nouns from the story. Complete the exercise with the adjectives which describe them.

(a) _____ daughter

(b) _____ floodwaters

(c) _____ couple

(d) _____ ending

(e) _____ site

(f) _____ brother

3. Writers often use alliteration (because words seem to run together more smoothly). For example, Peter Pan, the Wicked Witch of the West, Black Beauty. Write an example from the story.

_____

4. Complete the crossword puzzle. All answers are found in the story.

Across	Down
2. royal chair	1. killed
5. forced	3. dwelling
6. spouse	4. conclusion
8. sorrowful	7. angry
12. reared	9. monarch
13. powerful being	10. poor
15. certain	11. location
16. attempt	14. conflict

This classic story from France is a popular fantasy which has sold millions of books around the world. The author was a pilot who lost his life in World War II after winning medals for bravery. Portraits of the two main characters have appeared on French banknotes in recent years.

The Little Prince

Once there was a boy who didn't have a very good opinion of adults. When he grew up he became a pilot who, on a solo flight, crash-landed in the Sahara Desert. There, he met a strange child with golden hair who also had a poor opinion of grown-ups, for he had met many strange ones on his travels in space. The stranded airman learned that the child was a prince from a planet called Asteroid B612. The little prince had been lonely on his tiny planet with only a flower to talk to so he left. As the pilot tried to fix his damaged plane, he answered the child's many odd but interesting questions.

The little prince told his new companion about the baobab trees which threatened to destroy his home. He described how he had been roaming the universe in his search to find out what was really important in life. On this amazing journey he first met an old king on a different planet, on another he met a show-off who thought he was the handsomest, the most intelligent and the richest man on his planet, even though he was the only person there! On another planet he met a businessman who spent his time counting and recording the number of stars as if they were money. He also met a lamplighter, a signalman, a shopkeeper and an elderly gentleman who wrote enormous books.

After these meetings he decided adults were very strange people!

Finally, the prince reached Earth and his pilot friend, but, after many pleasant hours in each other's company, the child had an encounter with a venomous yellow snake.

Eventually the pilot repaired his engine and returned home to his friends. They were pleased to see him again but couldn't understand why he was sad.

I wonder why he was so unhappy?

Read this junior fiction book:

The Little Prince – A. De Saint-Exupery

The Little Prince

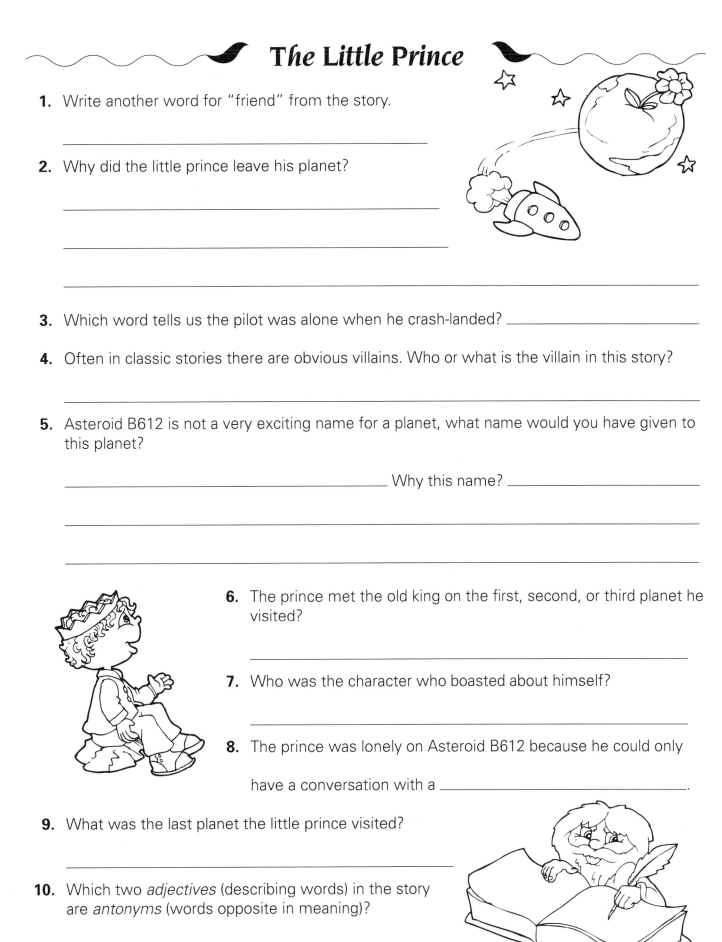

1. Write another word for "friend" from the story.

   _____

2. Why did the little prince leave his planet?

   _____

   _____

3. Which word tells us the pilot was alone when he crash-landed? _____

4. Often in classic stories there are obvious villains. Who or what is the villain in this story?

   _____

5. Asteroid B612 is not a very exciting name for a planet, what name would you have given to this planet?

   _____ Why this name? _____

   _____

   _____

6. The prince met the old king on the first, second, or third planet he visited?

   _____

7. Who was the character who boasted about himself?

   _____

8. The prince was lonely on Asteroid B612 because he could only

   have a conversation with a _____.

9. What was the last planet the little prince visited?

   _____

10. Which two *adjectives* (describing words) in the story are *antonyms* (words opposite in meaning)?

    _____

The Little Prince

1. The Little Prince was trying to discover which things in life are the most important. List *three* things which you think are the most important. With your teacher, organize a chalkboard tally and find out the top three choices made by the class.

   1. _____ 2. _____ 3. _____

2. Shade the boxes containing adjectives which describe the prince.

cruel	lonely	boring	blonde
adventurous	elderly	curious	

3. Number these events in correct time order.

   (a) The pilot fixed his engine. ☐

   (b) The prince met a businessman. ☐

   (c) The pilot met the little prince. ☐

   (d) The little prince reached Earth. ☐

   (e) The pilot's friends were pleased to see him. ☐

4. Asteroid B612 is not a very interesting name for a planet. Use your library to discover where the planets in our solar system got their names from and complete the retrieval chart.

Planet	Origin of name
Jupiter	
Mars	
Venus	
Uranus	
Neptune	
Saturn	
Mercury	
Pluto	

   What did you discover about the origin of the names?

   _____

   _____

5. This is a baobab tree which grows on the Little Prince's planet. Use reference books and write two sentences about baobab trees.

   _____

   _____

   _____

A.A. Milne was a famous English author and poet best known for his children's books. He based the characters in his classic Pooh stories on the stuffed toys belonging to his son, Christopher Robin. Milne was born in London and attended Cambridge University.

Winnie the Pooh

There are many stories about Winnie-the-Pooh who, though he thinks he is unintelligent, is a very kind bear. He is also known as Edward Bear to his friend, Christopher Robin. In these tales, the rather plump little bear has many adventures in and around the Hundred Acre Wood with his animal friends. These include a young pig named Piglet, Eeyore, an old grey donkey and the lively Tigger who thinks he is the only tiger in the world until he sees his reflection in a mirror! There is also a rather grumpy owl who uses Eeyore's lost tail as a bell rope, a clever rabbit and Kanga, the mother of Baby Roo.

In one adventure, Pooh wants to catch a heffalump. He and Piglet decide on a deep pit with a honey jar at the bottom to entice their prey. While Pooh goes home for the honey, Piglet prepares the trap. They leave, intending to return the following morning to see how many heffalumps they have caught. However, Pooh is hungry during the night and when he finds nothing in his larder he remembers the honey in Piglet's pit. Piglet also decides to visit the deep hole to see his first heffalump. On hearing noises from the trap he thinks they have caught one but it turns out to be Pooh Bear who is rolling around noisily, trying to pull the honey jar off his head!

Other adventures include the playing of Pooh-sticks, a simple game invented by Pooh, a hunt for a woozle and a comical mistake by Pooh and Piglet when they build a house for Eeyore.

You will enjoy reading about these and many other adventures.

Read one of these junior fiction books:

The Complete Tales of Winnie the Pooh – A.A. Milne
The House at Pooh Corner – A.A. Milne

Winnie the Pooh

1. What place for storing food is mentioned in the story?

_____

2. Who dug the pit to catch a heffalump?

_____

3. What game did Pooh Bear invent?

_____

4. Why did Pooh return to the pit at night?

_____

5. The honey jar is stuck on Piglet's head.
True or False?

_____

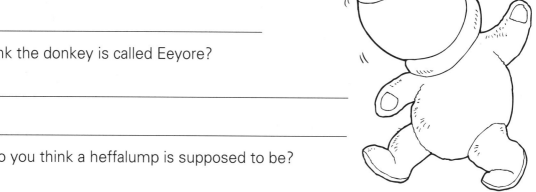

6. Why do you think the donkey is called Eeyore?

_____

_____

7. Which animal do you think a heffalump is supposed to be?

_____

Why? _____

_____

8. What was used to attract the heffalump to the pit? _____

9. (a) In the first paragraph there are two antonyms (words opposite in meaning).
What are they?

_____

_____

(b) In the second paragraph, there are two antonyms.
What are they?

_____

_____

1. Use your imagination and describe in a few sentences what you think a heffalump looks like. Then use your description to draw or paint it.

_____

_____

_____

2. Shade the boxes containing adjectives which describe Pooh Bear.

cruel	popular	kind
tubby	huge	brainy

3. Verbs are usually action words. Select the correct verb to complete each of these phrases from the passage.

(a) _____ the trap

(b) _____ the honey

(c) _____ a house

(d) _____ by Pooh

(e) _____ around noisily

(f) _____ his reflection

4. Complete the cloze passage based on the story. Use only *one* word in each space.

In these popular stories by A.A. Milne, we meet an old grey _____

and a clever _____. We hear how _____ wants to catch a

strange _____ called a heffalump with the _____ of his tiny

friend Piglet. He is unable to _____ and after getting up he feels

_____ but finds no _____ in his larder. He then decides to eat

some _____ from the large _____ for his head becomes

_____ inside the jar and as he is _____ around the pit

_____.

The Legend of Robin Hood

Robin Hood and his men in Lincoln green lived in Sherwood Forest near Nottingham. Robin had been outlawed for killing a deer belonging to Prince John but was a hero to the poor.

The prince had seized his brother's throne while King Richard the Lionheart was overseas fighting to free Jerusalem from the Saracens.

Over the years, Robin had gathered together a fine band of fighting men. There was Little John who had defeated Robin in a fight with quarterstaves. Alan-A-Dale, a wandering minstrel singing sad songs, joined Robin because he'd lost his future wife to an aged wealthy knight.

With Robin's help he rescued his bride-to-be and everyone celebrated at a wedding feast in Sherwood Forest.

Friar Tuck, a splendid swordsman, and Will Scarlet both fought Robin and impressed him so much he invited them to join his outlaw band.

After many attempts to capture Robin, the Sheriff of Nottingham decided to hold an archery contest to attract the best bowman in the land. The winner's prize was an arrow made of gold and silver. Robin, in disguise, entered and was victorious but when discovered, he and his men had to flee.

When King Richard returned from overseas he had to decide whether to arrest Robin. Richard and his soldiers dressed up as monks and entered the forest.

Would he see Robin as an evil outlaw who should be arrested or a loyal subject who deserved his freedom?

Read this junior fiction book:

Robin Hood – a version illustrated by M. Early

1. Who were the "men in Lincoln green"?

_____

2. Which word tells us Robin won the archery contest?

_____

3. What is the name given to long sticks used as weapons?

_____

4. Write synonyms from the story for these words:

(a) dwelt _____ (b) grabbed _____

(c) assistance _____ (d) wicked _____

(e) faithful _____ (f) archer _____

5. Why didn't the sheriff's men recognize Robin when he entered the archery contest?

_____

6. If King Richard had found Robin in the forest, what do you think he would have done?

_____

7. Which word in the story describes a person who roams the land singing songs and reciting poems?

_____

8. Why do you think King Richard was called "the Lionheart"?

_____

_____

9. What color were the clothes worn by Robin's men?

_____

10. Why was Robin branded an outlaw?

_____

_____

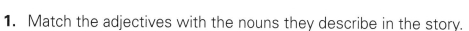

Robin Hood

1. Match the adjectives with the nouns they describe in the story.

Adjectives	Nouns
(a) fine •	• subject
(b) loyal •	• minstrel
(c) many •	• knight
(d) splendid •	• Robin
(e) evil •	• band
(f) victorious •	• adventures
(g) wandering •	• swordsman
(h) aged •	• outlaw

2. View the video *The Adventures of Robin Hood* with Errol Flynn. List several characters to complete the box below. Then write a comment about each film character chosen.

Character	Comment

3. In the stories about Robin Hood, he fought against Norman knights. William the Conqueror was the leader in the Norman conquest of Britain. Use reference books and write a few sentences about him.

4. Archery contests have been held throughout history. Read about "archery" in your library and write about it using these guidelines:

   (a)   Briefly outline the history and show when bows were first used.

   (b)   Describe the target used in contests and the scoring system.

   (c)   List the equipment used by a member of an archery club.

   (d)   Draw and label a diagram of a longbow.

   (e)   Use your phone book and name the closest archery club to your home.

Classical Literature   *World Teachers Press®*

How the World was Created

This Chinese myth tells us that in the beginning all was in darkness with no night and day. There were no animals, no birds hovering on high and no trees or flowers. It was a sad world indeed!

Pan Ku, the Earth's first creature, slept through this silent darkness for thousands of years. After waking up, he grew into a huge giant. Later, the world's lighter sections floated upwards to become the sky and the heavy parts sank to become the land. Because of this split there was daylight throughout the whole world.

As Pan Ku grew taller, he continually pushed the sky upwards away from the land so that they would never again join together and bring back the gloom. Wanting to make the world a more attractive place, Pan Ku spent his life patiently digging out deep valleys, building massive mountains and creating seas. Exhausted by this difficult work and by constantly pushing up the sky, the giant had to stop his labors and eventually lie down to die.

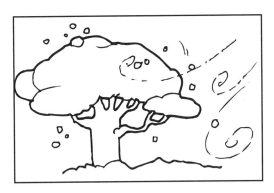

Pan Ku's final breaths became the winds and the clouds, and his voice turned into thunder. His eyes became the sun and the moon. The giant's arms and legs became mountain ranges and his blood the rivers. The hairs on his body became plants, his tears rain and his bones sank into the ground. I wonder what his bones became?

Some Chinese thought Pan Ku's life did not really end for his body parts were all around them in different forms and because his eyes were up in the heavens, he still watched over his people below.

How the World was Created

1. Why did some Chinese think that Pan Ku was still alive?

_____

_____

2. Where did the moon come from?

_____

3. Give a single word for "arms and legs." _____

4. Which of the giant's body parts became trees?

_____

5. Authors often use alliteration because the words then seem to run together more smoothly, e.g., the <u>W</u>icked <u>W</u>itch of the <u>W</u>est. Give an example of alliteration from the story.

_____

6. Select synonyms from the story for these words.

    (a)   excavating _____

    (b)   last _____

    (c)   enormous _____

    (d)   tired _____

    (e)   constructing _____

    (f)   legend _____

7. What caused the giant's death?

_____

8. Why did Pan Ku keep pushing the land and the sky apart?

_____

9. "Continually" means carrying on without any pauses. What other word in the story has a

similar meaning? _____

10. What do you think the giant's bones became?

_____

1. The words listed below are adjectives (describing words) used in the story. Write the noun each one describes.

(a) silent _____ (b) massive _____

(c) Chinese _____ (d) first _____

(e) lighter _____ (f) sad _____

2. Draw or paint a picture that suits this story.

3. Complete the crossword puzzle. All answers are found in the story.

Across	**Down**
4. darkness	1. everything
6. slumbered	2. not shallow
9. mountain chains	3. cease
11. perish	5. a satellite
12. unhappy	6. soundless
13. legend	7. conclude
15. enormous	8. animal
16. after a while	10. dales
17. beneath	14. weighty

4. The giant Pan Ku slept for thousands of years. In a famous Washington Irving story, **Rip Van Winkle** slept for 20 years. An old European folk tale tells how **Sleeping Beauty** slept for 100 years. Use reference materials and write a few sentences about each of the characters.

5. List some of the changes you think you would see if you awoke after sleeping for 100 years.

_____

_____

_____

Greek legends with their mythical heroes have been told for thousands of years. They helped the ancient Greeks to explain why the sun crossed the sky, why storms raged at sea and how their lives were watched over by the gods who lived on Mount Olympus.

The Wooden Horse of Troy

Many years ago the soldiers of Greece fought a 10-year war against King Priam, ruler of the city of Troy. Paris, Priam's handsome son, had stolen Helen, the beautiful young wife of Menelaus who was the old ruler of the Greek kingdom of Sparta. An angry Menelaus gathered together a large army of fifty thousand men led by Odysseus, Achilles and Ajax, famous warriors of Greek legends. Soon, the fleet of a thousand ships set sail for Troy and lay siege to the ancient city defended by Hector, the greatest of Trojan heroes.

After years of fighting, Paris and several of the great soldier princes were dead, but the Greek army could not breach the high city walls. Then the wise Odysseus devised a clever plan. He had a huge wooden horse built, which was left outside the city walls. The Greeks then launched their ships and pretended to sail away.

Inside the city, the Trojans were delighted and celebrated because they thought the long war was finally over. They believed the enormous horse had been left as a gift so it was hauled inside the city gates. After the celebrations were over, night fell and the citizens went to sleep, unaware that Greek warriors were hiding inside the horse's stomach. Under cover of darkness, these men crept out of hiding and opened the city gates. In poured the Greek army from the ships which had returned to the shore. Was Helen rescued at last after years of war and the loss of so many lives?

Read one of these junior fiction books:

Greek Myths – G. McCaughrean
The Trojan Horse: How the Greeks Won the War – E. Little

The Wooden Horse of Troy

1. In the passage a large number of ships is a _____.

2. How long did the Trojan war last?

   _____

3. Why was Menelaus angry?

   _____

   _____

   _____

4. Which word in the story means "to break through"? _____

5. What are the citizens of the city of Troy called? _____

6. Who was the great warrior who defended Troy? _____

7. Why did the citizens of Troy celebrate?

   _____

   _____

   _____

8. Adjectives are words which describe nouns. Which noun do the adjectives "young" and "beautiful" describe?

   _____

9. Which word tells us the citizens of Troy did not know Greek warriors were hiding inside the wooden horse?

   _____

10. How do you think the story of Helen of Troy ends?

    _____

    _____

    _____

    _____

The Wooden Horse of Troy

1. Helen of Troy is often referred to as "the face that launched a thousand ships."
   Explain this description in your own words.

_____

_____

2. Number these events in the correct time order.

   (a)   The Greeks built a wooden horse. ☐   (b)   Greek ships sailed away. ☐

   (c)   Menelaus gathered an army. ☐   (d)   The people of Troy celebrated. ☐

   (e)   Hidden Greeks opened the city gates. ☐

3. Use adjectives (describing words) from the passage to complete the blanks in this cloze.

The _____ ruler of Sparta gathered a _____ army led by

_____ warriors of _____ legends. They attacked the

_____ city of Troy but couldn't get past the _____ city

walls. Soon the _____ Odysseus had worked out a

_____ plan. It was successful but the _____

Paris and several _____ soldier princes lost their lives.

4. Use reference books in your library and write a sentence about each
   Greek god, goddess or hero listed on the chart.

Name	Sentence
Jason	
Heracles	
Athena	
Theseus	
Ajax	
Hermes	
Zeus	
Poseidon	

The Selfish Giant

While a giant is away for seven years visiting another ogre, local schoolchildren play in his beautiful castle garden. In spring they play games under peach blossoms and among flowers as birds sing in the trees. But soon their enjoyment ends, for the giant returns.

Wanting his garden to himself, the giant chases the children away and builds a wall around his land. He erects a notice saying "Trespassers will be prosecuted." However, when spring and summer come around again in the rest of the country, it remains winter in the garden. As there are no happy children there, the trees forget to blossom and no birds sing.

The giant is miserable for now it is always winter with its snow and frost. Then one day he hears the song of a finch and looking outside he sees birds, blossoms and flowers. He realizes that the children have crept back into his garden through a hole in the wall and brought spring with them. The giant is delighted! He helps a tearful little boy and knocks down his wall.

Now the children play in the garden once more, but the giant's favorite little boy is never seen. Years later, when the giant is very old and frail, the boy appears again. The child says he has come to reward the giant's kindness by welcoming him to his garden. The giant is pleased to see his young friend again and the ending is both joyful and sad.

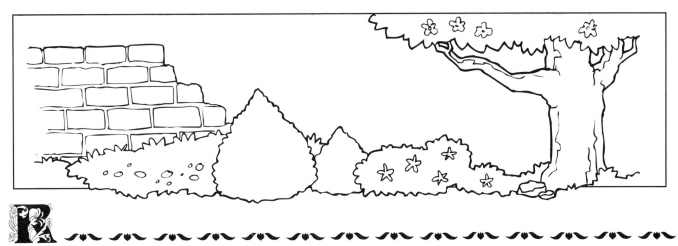

Read one of these junior fiction books:

The Selfish Giant – a version with illustrations by S.S. Gallagher
The Selfish Giant – a version with illustrations by Lisbeth Zwerger
The Giant's Garden – a version by L.W. Gilbert

The Selfish Giant

1. Which word tells us the giant didn't like the cold weather?

_____

2. What kinds of trees grew in the giant's garden?

_____

3. What kind of home did the giant have?

_____

4. What is a finch? _____

_____

5. Why is the giant described as a selfish giant?

_____

_____

6. Which word describes people who go on
other people's property without permission?

_____

7. From the story, find another word for giant.

_____

8. The giant has learned that being _____ is better than being

_____ .

9. Why did the birds stop singing?

_____

_____

_____

10. Why does the giant knock down the garden walls?

_____

_____

World Teachers Press®

# The Selfish Giant

1. Number these events in the story in time order.

(a)   The giant builds a wall.   ☐

(b)   Trees forget to blossom.   ☐

(c)   The giant visits a friend.   ☐

(d)   The children are chased away.   ☐

(e)   Children crawl through a hole.   ☐

(f)   The little boy appears again years later.   ☐

2. Synonyms are words which are similar in meaning. Find synonyms from the story for the words in the crossword puzzle.

Across	Down
2. finishes	1. beneath
3. uncaring	4. contented
5. emerges	6. pleased
7. plants	8. shortly
9. pleasure	9. conclusion
14. elderly	10. cheerful
15. sneaked	11. blemishes
16. warble	12. observes
17. assists	13. companion

3. Draw or paint your own picture showing the things that could be seen in the garden in spring.

4. Listen to the "Hodder Children's Audio Tape" available from your public library. This contains six of Wilde's fairy tales, including *The Selfish Giant*.

Jules Verne was born in France in 1828. In his adventure books he often anticipates the scientific inventions of a later time. This story has proved to be one of his most successful.

The Mysterious Island

In 1865, a balloon with five men on board is caught in a violent storm above the Pacific Ocean. The men, loyal to the northern, anti-slavery states during the American Civil War, have escaped from a Confederate prison camp. Their captured balloon has been carried thousands of kilometers out to sea by strong winds. They manage to reach an island, which they later name Lincoln Island after their president, but they think they have lost their leader, Captain Harding. However, his dog, Top, leads them to its master, who wonders how he has reached dry land when he was drowning in deep water far out at sea!

Using their leader's scientific knowledge, the castaways manage to make clay bricks to build a shelter, tools from iron melted in hot fires, explosives from a mixture of various chemicals, candles using seal fat and a canoe to explore the lonely island's shores.

The men soon settle down in their new home under the Southern Cross. When they find a seaman's chest containing clothes, guns, pans and a telescope, they have all they want. They even have a tamed orangutan called Jupiter for a servant—but need to keep a watchful eye on the dormant volcano that towers above the island.

Then, of course, apart from Harding's miraculous rescue, other odd happenings occur often and can't be explained. They find a bullet in a wild pig they eat, but there's no one else on the island! A message in a floating bottle helps them to rescue a sailor marooned on a nearby island. He confesses to murder and piracy but says he did not send the bottle! Later, when they defend the island against pirates, the pirate ship is destroyed in a huge explosion and several pirates who reach the shore are found dead without a scratch on them! Perhaps you can find the answer to these mysterious events.

Read this junior fiction book:

The Mysterious Island – J. Verne

The Mysterious Island

1. Which word from the passage means people who are stranded on an island?

   _____

2. Which animal provided the fat for making candles?

   _____

3. The island is in the northern hemisphere. True or False?

   _____

4. What kind of war is one where soldiers from the same country fight each other?

   _____

5. Which word from the story tells us that the volcano is not extinct and could erupt at any time?

   _____

6. Where did the men find the telescope?

   _____

7. How did the men find their leader, Captain Harding?

   _____

8. Why do you think the book is called *The Mysterious Island*?

   _____

   _____

9. Did the Confederate army fight for the northern or the southern states of America?

   _____

10. Who or what do you think killed the pirates who reached the island?

   _____

   _____

11. Captain Harding figured out that Lincoln Island was 48 km long and 16 km wide. Draw what you think the island looked like and show the following information.

   (a) The island is under the Southern Cross, so rule in the Equator.
   (b) Mark with a red cross their first camp site on the beach.
   (c) Show Union Bay and Washington Bay.
   (d) Show the volcano they named Franklin Mountain.
   (e) Show the cliffs along the rocky coast and the lake on top of the cliffs.
   (f) Draw in the Mercy River (which flows along the foot of the cliffs where they lived in a cave) and the bridge they built over the river.
       Remember to show your symbols in a legend.

The Mysterious Island

1. Use reference materials to write a paragraph on the American Civil War.

2. Which nouns in the story do these adjectives describe?

(a) violent _____   (b) hot _____

(c) dry _____   (d) wild _____

(e) huge _____   (f) strong _____

3. Complete the crossword puzzle. All answers are in the story.

Across

1. protect
9. isolated
11. over
16. vessel
22. pots
25. frequently
28. mariner
31. beneath

6. arrived
10. devour
12. not shallow
17. metal
23. transported
27. boat
30. leader

Down

2. discover
4. airship
7. enormous
13. gaol
15. untamed
19. seized
21. sleeping
26. dispatch

3. arid
5. name
8. lifeless
14. coast
18. strange
20. mark
24. happenings
29. conflict

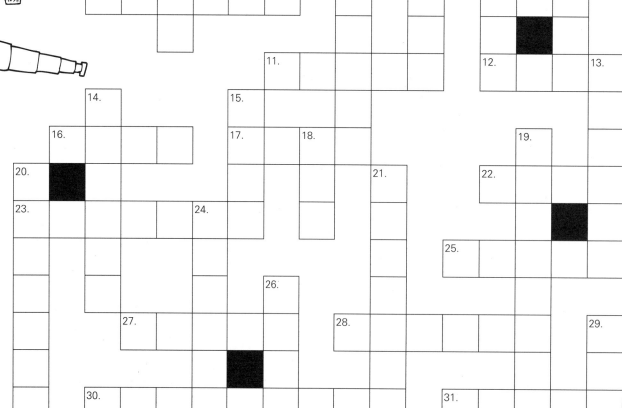

The Rainbow Serpent

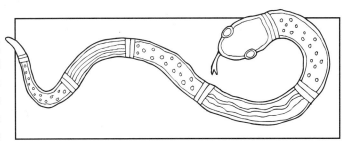

The most widespread belief among Aboriginal people is about the existence of a huge, brilliantly colored serpent with long red and yellow stripes along its body. In remote caves all around Australia there are red ochre paintings of the Rainbow Serpent and experts believe they have been there for thousands of years.

The giant snake, regarded as female among the Aboriginal people of northern Australia, rests in waterholes in the dry season and its tracks created rivers as it slithered along during the Dreaming. In the wet season, it is seen in the sky as a rainbow. It swallows people who break the laws and causes natural disasters like floods and droughts.

Many creation stories tell of the serpent's anger when roused from sleep, so Aboriginal people take care not to disturb it. The Gunwinggu people relate the story of an orphan boy whose constant crying angers the snake. Another story describes how the resting snake is disturbed so it seizes and swallows a dingo, fortunately warning some Aboriginal children playing and swimming in the waterhole on a hot day. The members of the Murrinpatha tribe tell how the serpent helps its friends, the flying foxes, to fight a bat and a toad-fish. A legend from northern Australia, an area with frequent thunderstorms, explains how hailstones are the eggs of the Rainbow Serpent. The hailstones burrow slowly into the ground and become worms, the children of the snake.

The Rainbow Serpent still affects the lives of Aboriginal people today as they defend its right to lie at rest and be undisturbed by modern building projects. Perhaps this belief could be discussed with your class.

The Rainbow Serpent

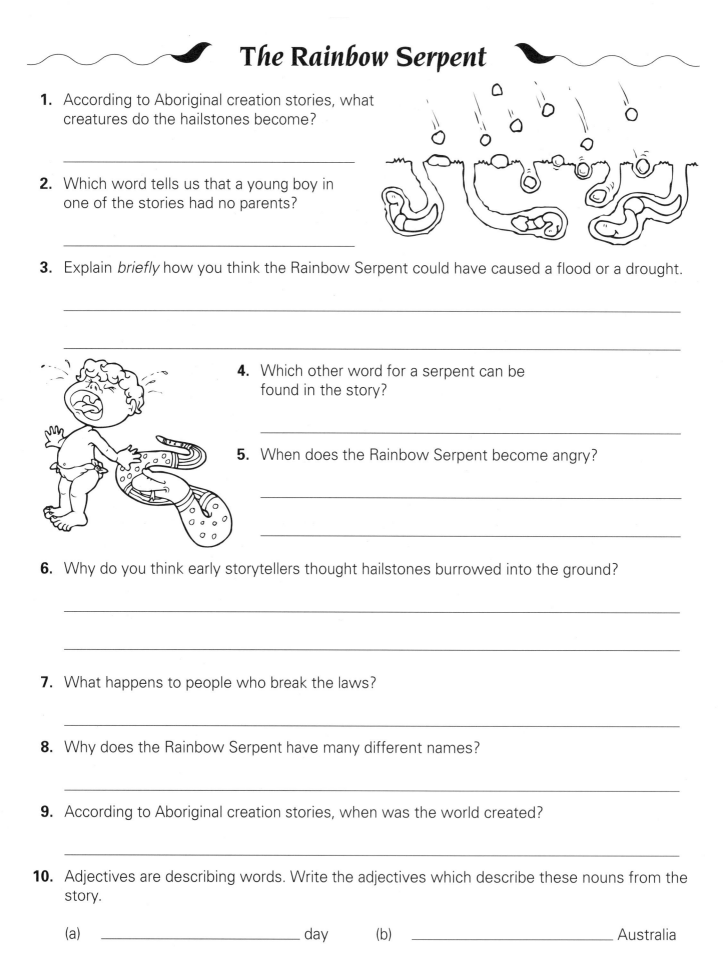

1. According to Aboriginal creation stories, what creatures do the hailstones become?

   _____

2. Which word tells us that a young boy in one of the stories had no parents?

   _____

3. Explain *briefly* how you think the Rainbow Serpent could have caused a flood or a drought.

   _____

   _____

4. Which other word for a serpent can be found in the story?

   _____

5. When does the Rainbow Serpent become angry?

   _____

   _____

6. Why do you think early storytellers thought hailstones burrowed into the ground?

   _____

   _____

7. What happens to people who break the laws?

   _____

8. Why does the Rainbow Serpent have many different names?

   _____

9. According to Aboriginal creation stories, when was the world created?

   _____

10. Adjectives are describing words. Write the adjectives which describe these nouns from the story.

    (a) _____ day   (b) _____ Australia

    (c) _____ disasters   (d) _____ stories

Classical Literature   World Teachers Press®

The Rainbow Serpent

T	C	O	B	R	A	C	N
P	Y	T	H	O	N	O	L
S	M	D	B	P	A	S	P
U	B	U	V	U	C	P	M
G	R	G	I	G	O	T	A
T	A	I	P	A	N	H	M
B	S	T	E	S	D	C	B
R	P	E	R	L	A	O	A

1. The giant snake in Australian Aboriginal creation stories hides in waterholes during the dry season. Find the snakes hiding in this word search.

   (a) ___ ___ ___ P A ___   (b) ___ ___ M B ___

   (c) ___ ___ B R ___   (d) ___ I P ___ ___

   (e) ___ ___ T H ___ ___   (f) ___ U G ___ ___ ___

   (g) ___ S ___   (h) ___ ___ ___ C O ___ ___ ___

   Now use a reference book and write a sentence about one of the snakes.

   _____

   _____

2. Use these words to complete the cloze passage.

   whole   creature   different   tales   lives   Dreaming   rests   modern   thought   rivers

   Many _____ about a giant snake are told by _____

   Aboriginal people throughout the _____ of Australia. The huge snake

   _____ in the dry season and is _____ to have created

   _____ during the ancient _____. The _____ still

   affects the _____ of Aboriginal people in _____ times.

3. Using some elements from traditional Aboriginal painting (for example, earth-colored dots, strongly colored lines, circles) draw and paint your own Rainbow Serpent in a design which includes other Australian animals.

4. We use *similes* in order to compare one thing with another and give a clearer description. For example, the mouse is *as light as a feather;* he is as *fast as lightning.*
   Use your own similes to describe these creatures from the story.

   (a)   the worms were as _____

   (b)   the dingo is as _____

   (c)   the snake was as _____

   (d)   the flying foxes are as _____

Kipling was an English novelist who was born in India, which is the setting for some of his books. These animal stories were first published in 1902 and were based on those Kipling told his daughter, Josephine. Rudyard Kipling is buried in Poets' Corner in Westminster Abbey.

How the Whale got his Throat

This is a story about a whale which eats fish until there is only one small fish left in the ocean. This fish is a 'Stute fish which has always swum behind the whale's right ear so it can't be seen.

One day, when the whale is hungry, the tiny fish suggests that men are tasty and tells the enormous cetacean where it can find a shipwrecked mariner on a raft. The whale finds the solitary seaman and swallows him, his raft and his knife. Once inside the whale the trapped sailor dances the hornpipe and leaps around. He bites, crawls about and even yells loudly. This makes the whale very uncomfortable and gives it the hiccups. When it asks the seaman to come out he refuses unless the whale agrees to take him home to Britain, once called Albion.

The gigantic sea creature eventually agrees and the sailor walks out onto the beach. He leaves behind a square, wooden grating which he pulls into place with his suspenders, which had held up his breeches. This carved grating is wedged tightly in the whale's throat and means that it cannot eat men or women or girls or boys, only small fish.

The clever seaman goes home to his mother, marries and lives happily ever after. However, the 'Stute fish is afraid that the huge whale may be angry with him. I wonder what the tiny fish decides to do?

Read one of these junior fiction books:

Just So Stories – Rudyard Kipling
The Complete Just So Stories – Rudyard Kipling

# How the Whale got his Throat

1. Give two other words for "seaman" from the story.

   _____   _____

2. What do you think the seaman used to carve out the wooden grating?

   _____

3. How can you tell this story is a fantasy in which wildly imaginative things happen?

   _____

   _____

   _____

4. Where do you think the wood for the carved grating came from?

   _____

5. From the story, give the name of the dance once popular with sailors.

   _____

6. What was once another name for Britain?

   _____

7. Why can't the whale eat people now?

   _____

   _____

8. Which word in the story can be used to describe the group of sea mammals which includes whales, porpoises and dolphins?

   _____

9. Find three words from the story which mean very big.

   _____

   _____

   _____

10. The last fish in the sea was a 'Stute fish. I think the author was having a joke with his readers. Find the meaning of the word "astute." Why do you think Kipling called the fish by this name?

    _____

    _____

How the Whale got his Throat

1. This tale from the "Just So" stories tells us why the whale has a small throat. Write your own brief animal fable telling how the elephant got its trunk, or the camel its hump, or the leopard its spots, etc.

2. The 'Stute fish is an odd name. See if you can find these other strangely named fish in the word search. Some of these fish are mentioned in the original story. The answers are jumbled.

S	S	A	L	M	O	N
O	X	D	L	I	N	G
L	S	A	B	N	D	P
E	K	B	X	N	A	I
H	A	D	D	O	C	K
O	T	N	W	W	E	E
T	E	S	P	R	A	T

(a) LESO _____

(b) TKSAE _____

(c) NASMOL _____

(d) NGIL _____

(e) BDA _____

(f) KEPI _____

(g) PTSAR _____

(h) CDEA _____

(i) DDKOCHA _____

(j) NNMWOI _____

3. Rudyard Kipling was the first British writer to be awarded the Nobel Prize for Literature. Use your library to research and write a few sentences about the Nobel prizes.

_____

_____

_____

_____

_____

_____

_____

4. *The Elephant's Child* is another of the "Just So" stories and there is a video, narrated by famous actor Jack Nicholson, available at public libraries. Watch the video and then write a review of the film for a friend who hasn't seen it.

These stories, written by Norman Hunter, first appeared in the 1920s in a children's magazine and were later broadcast by the British Broadcasting Corporation. The books have been translated into many languages including French, Italian, German and Chinese. Written over the next 40 years, more stories about the absent-minded professor have been enjoyed by children all over the world.

The Incredible Adventures of Professor Branestawm

Professor Branestawm is an eccentric inventor who lives in the town of Great Pagwell. He is bald and on his high-domed forehead he wears five pairs of glasses. Each pair is used for a different purpose—one is even used to look for the others when he loses them! He has very few friends for he talks to them like a teacher and they don't understand a lot of the difficult words he uses. Many of his inventions are not too successful!

One invention is a time machine which he shows to Colonel Dedshott of the Catapult Cavaliers. They climb into the machine and move back in time to a country where rebels win a battle to overthrow their king. However, his invention has changed history, for the professor remembers that the king's soldiers actually won the battle!

Branestawm also invents a burglar catcher as thieves have stolen his silver teapot (a gift from his aunt) and other valued items. Then one night the professor goes to see a film about the home life of brussels sprouts. Returning home he realizes he has left his key inside the house. He climbs in through the window and is caught by his own burglar catcher!

His jellyfish-catching equipment and his machines for making pancakes and peeling potatoes all lead the inventor into trouble. These are just a few of his incredible adventures. Many more tales, such as the story about his fight with a ferocious pudding, can be enjoyed in other books about this unusual professor!

The Incredible Adventures of Professor Branestawm

1. From the story, write the adjectives which describe these nouns.

(a) _____ pudding (b) _____ teapot

(c) _____ words (d) _____ inventor

2. Why did the professor invent a burglar catcher?

_____

3. Who traveled in the time machine? _____

4. Why doesn't the professor have many friends?

_____

5. What gift did one of the professor's relatives give him? _____

6. Give your own reason why the professor had to fight a ferocious pudding.

_____

_____

7. Which word in the passage means "fierce"? _____

8. What mistake did the time machine make?

_____

9. Professor Branestawm is a schoolteacher. True or False?_____

10. The professor left his key inside the house. What else tells us he is rather careless?

_____

_____

11. Professor Branestawm's inventions were often unsuccessful! Match these inventors to their very successful inventions. You will need to use your library.

(a) Guglielmo Marconi (Italy)　●　　　●　Powered Plane 1903
(b) Alexander G. Bell (USA)　●　　　●　Gas Engine 1885
(c) Samuel Colt (USA)　●　　　●　Pneumatic Tire 1887
(d) William Roentgen (Germany)　●　　　●　Writing for the Blind 1826
(e) John Dunlop (Britain)　●　　　●　Revolver 1831
(f) Gottlieb Daimler (Germany)　●　　　●　Telephone 1876
(g) Alfred Nobel (Sweden)　●　　　●　Radio 1895
(h) Louis Braille (France)　●　　　●　X-Rays 1895
(i) Robert Watson Watt (Britain)　●　　　●　Radar 1935
(j) Wright Brothers (USA)　●　　　●　Dynamite 1866

Pippi Longstocking 6 – 8

Page 7
1. the townspeople
2. strong enough to lift her horse; defeats the circus strongman in a wrestling match
3. orphan
4. an area for growing fruit trees
5. Pippi, Tommy, Annika and Mr. Nelson
6. heroine
7. in preparation for his retirement
8. they are her next-door neighbors
9. forces them to dance the polka until the early hours of the morning
10. a bull

Page 8
1. Teacher check
2. (a) 2   (b) 5   (c) 1   (d) 3   (e) 4
3. (b), (c) and (e)
4. Teacher check
   Because she is so **strong** and can **lift** a horse, Pippi is an **unusual** girl. She has a **monkey** for a friend and it **sits** on her shoulder. The townspeople **think** that Pippi should not live **alone** but she does not **agree** with them. At the **circus** Pippi upsets some of the performers but people in the **audience** love her.

William Tell 9 – 11

Page 10
1. tyrant
2. because he was popular
3. bow to his hat in the market square
4. people not bowing to his hat; Tell's secret plan to kill him
5. close-fitting, sleeveless jacket
6. governor
7. pleased – furious/horrified released – arrested
8. those who disobeyed Gessler
9. he had a second arrow to kill Gessler if he missed and slew his own son
10. they would be stronger so they could defend themselves against invaders

Page 11
1. William's son. He was brave and believed in his father's ability to strike the apple
2. Teacher check
3.

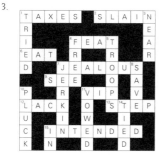

4. The Lone Ranger

The Song of Hiawatha 12 – 14

Page 13
1. lake
2. lodge
3. oak, birch, pine, ash
4. his father deserted him and his mother; his mother died of a broken heart
5. wigwam, tepee
6. Iagoo
7. lapping of the waves, language of birds and animals

8. the animals
9. (a) leather shoes
   (b) gloves without fingers
10. brave

Page 14
1. Teacher check
2.

	cruel	old	brave	caring	strong	lovely	skilled	knowledgeable	young	sad
Hiawatha			✔			✔	✔	✔		
Mudjekeewis	✔									
Nokomis		✔		✔		✔		✔		
Megissogwon	✔		✔		✔					
Iagoo			✔			✔	✔			
Wenowah										✔

3. (a) village   (b) canoe   (c) forest
   (d) hunt   (e) language   (e) warrior

4.

|H| |C|E|L|E|B|R|A|T|E|S|
E		U							I		
L	E	T	S		T				M		
P		W	E	E	P	S			I		A
		L			P	U	D		I		N
				F	I	E	R	C	E		N
B	A	T	T	L	E		C				I
		V			N	E	S	T			T
D	E	A	D		H		R		R		R
	S	E		I			S	L	A	Y	S
		E		D				I			
G	U	A	R	D	E	D		F	L	O	W

Romulus and Remus 15 – 17

Page 16
1. Numitor
2. Romulus, Remus
3. false
4. Teacher check
5. ordered, commanded
6. Numitor
7. Amulius, Teacher check
8. due to rising flood waters
9. Mars, god of war
10. Teacher check

Page 17
1. Paris   – Seine
   New York   – Hudson
   London   – Thames
   Cairo   – Nile
   Melbourne   – Yarra
   Washington D.C. – Potomac
   Lisbon   – Tagus
2. (a) beautiful   (b) rising   (c) loving
   (d) sad   (e) chosen   (f) younger
3. humble home

4.

S		T	H	R	O	N	E		
L		O						E	
E		M	A	D	E			N	
W	I	F	E			S	A	D	
S		U	K					N	
	R	A	I	S	E	D			G	
I		I		N		E			
T		O		E			W		
E				G	O	D		A	
S	U	R	E			T	R	Y	

The Little Prince 18 –20

Page 19
1. companion
2. he was lonely, searching for what was important in life
3. solo
4. the venomous yellow snake

5. Teacher check
6. first
7. the show-off
8. flower
9. Earth
10. tiny/enormous

Page 20
1. Teacher check
2. lonely, adventurous, curious
3. (a) 4   (b) 1   (c) 3   (d) 2   (e) 5
4. Jupiter   – The chief Roman god
   Mars   – Roman god of war
   Venus   – Roman goddess of love/ beauty
   Uranus   – Greek god of heavens
   Neptune   – Roman/Greek god of the sky
   Saturn   – Roman god of agriculture
   Mercury   – Roman messenger of the gods
   Pluto   – Roman god of the underworld
4. Planets are named after ancient gods.
5. Teacher check

Winnie-the-Pooh 21 –23

Page 22
1. larder
2. Piglet
3. Pooh-sticks
4. he was hungry
5. false
6. after the sound a donkey makes
7. Teacher check e.g. elephant
8. honey
9. (a) unintelligent/clever
   (b) leave/return

Page 23
1. Teacher check
2. popular, kind, tubby
3. (a) prepares   (b) remembers
   (c) build   (d) invented
   (e) rolling   (f) sees
4. In these popular stories by A.A. Milne we meet an old grey **donkey** and a clever **rabbit**. We hear how **Pooh** wants to catch a strange **creature/animal** called a heffalump with the **help** of his tiny friend Piglet. He is unable to **sleep** and after getting up he feels **hungry** but finds no **food** in his larder. He then decides to eat some **honey** from the large **jar** left in the **pit/trap**. This proves to be a big **mistake** for his head becomes **stuck** inside the jar and is rolling around noisily.

The Legend of Robin Hood 24 – 26

Page 25
1. Robin Hood's men
2. victorious
3. quarterstaves
4. (a) lived   (b) seized
   (c) help   (d) evil
   (e) loyal   (f) bowman
5. he was in disguise
6. Teacher check
7. minstrel
8. Teacher check
9. Lincoln green
10. he killed a deer belonging to Prince John

Page 26
1. (a) fine   – band
   (b) loyal   – subject
   (c) many   – adventures
   (d) splendid   – swordsman
   (e) evil   – outlaw

(f) victorious – Robin
(g) wandering – minstrel
(h) aged – knight
2. Teacher check
3. Teacher check
4. Teacher check

How the World was Created 27 – 29

Page 28
1. they believed he lived because his body parts became their world and he still watched over the people
2. his eye(s)
3. limbs
4. the hairs of his body
5. massive mountains/hovering on high
6. (a) digging   (d) exhausted
   (b) final   (e) building
   (c) massive/huge   (f) myth
7. he was exhausted from all the work
8. so they wouldn't join and bring back the gloom
9. constantly
10. Teacher check

Page 29
1. (a) darkness   (d) creature
   (b) mountains   (e) sections
   (c) myth   (f) world
2. Teacher check
3.

4. Teacher check
5. Teacher check

The Wooden Horse of Troy 30 – 32

Page 31
1. fleet
2. 10 years
3. Paris had stolen his young wife
4. breach
5. Trojans
6. Hector
7. they thought the war was over when the Greek fleet sailed away
8. wife
9. unaware
10. Teacher check

Page 32
1. Teacher check
2. (a) 2   (b) 3   (c) 1
   (d) 4   (e) 5
3. The **old** ruler of Sparta gathered a **large** army led by **famous** warriors of **Greek** legends. They attacked the **ancient** city of Troy but couldn't get past the **high** city walls. Soon the **wise** Odysseus had worked out a **clever** plan. It was successful but the **handsome** Paris and several **great** soldier princes lost their lives.
4. Teacher check

The Selfish Giant 33 – 35

Page 34
1. miserable
2. peach
3. castle
4. a bird
5. he wants his garden for himself
6. trespassers
7. ogre
8. kind, selfish
9. because there were no children in the garden
10. Teacher check

Page 35
1. (a) 3   (b) 4   (c) 1
   (d) 2   (e) 5   (f) 6
2.

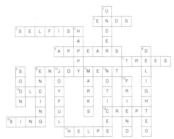

3. Teacher check
4. Teacher check

The Mysterious Island 36 – 38

Page 37
1. castaways
2. seal
3. false
4. civil
5. dormant
6. in a seaman's chest
7. his dog led them to him
8. Teacher check
9. southern
10. Teacher check
11. Teacher check

Page 38
1. Teacher check
2. (a) storm   (b) fires
   (c) land   (d) pig
   (e) explosion   (f) winds
3.

The Rainbow Serpent 39 – 41

Page 40
1. worms
2. orphan
3. Teacher check
4. snake
5. when it is disturbed
6. Teacher check

7. They are eaten by the serpent
8. Teacher check (Given different names by different groups)
9. during the Dreaming
10. (a) hot   (b) northern
    (c) natural   (d) creation/different

Page 41
1. (a) taipan   (b) mamba
   (c) cobra   (d) viper
   (e) python   (f) dugite
   (g) asp   (h) anaconda
   Teacher check
2. Many **tales** about a giant snake are told by **different** Aboriginal people throughout the **whole** of Australia. The huge snake **rests** in the dry season and is **thought** to have created **rivers** during the ancient **Dreaming**. The **creature** still affects the **lives** of Aboriginal people in **modern** times.
3. Teacher check
4. Teacher check

How the Whale got his Throat 42 – 44

Page 43
1. sailor, mariner
2. his knife
3. Teacher check
4. the raft
5. the hornpipe
6. Albion
7. its throat is too small as it is blocked by the grating
8. cetaceans
9. enormous, gigantic, huge
10. astute means clever; the fish is clever to avoid being eaten by the whale

Page 44
1. Teacher check
2. (a) sole   (b) skate   (c) salmon
   (d) ling   (e) dab   (f) pike
   (g) sprat   (h) dace   (j) haddock
   (j) minnow
3. Teacher check
4. Teacher check

The Incredible Adventures of Professor Branestawm 45 – 46

Page 46
1. (a) ferocious   (b) silver
   (c) difficult   (d) eccentric
2. thieves stole his silver teapot
3. Colonel Dedshott and the professor
4. he talks like a teacher/he uses words they don't understand
5. a silver teapot
6. Teacher check
7. ferocious
8. changed history
9. false
10. he had a pair of glasses to use when he lost his other four pairs
11. (a) Guglielmo Marconi – Radio 1895
    (b) Alexander G Bell – Telephone 1876
    (c) Samuel Colt – Revolver 1831
    (d) William Roentgen – X-Rays 1895
    (e) John Dunlop – Pneumatic Tire 1887
    (f) Gottlieb Daimler – Gas Engine 1885
    (g) Alfred Nobel – Dynamite 1866
    (h) Louis Braille – Writing for the Blind 1826
    (i) Robert Watson Watt – Radar 1935
    (j) Wright Brothers – Powered Plane 1903